Principles of
DIGITAL MARKETING

Principles of
DIGITAL MARKETING

---

7 KEYS TO ONLINE SUCCESS
IN TODAY'S INFORMATION ECONOMY
2nd Edition

J CHRISTIAN CONNETT

Library of Congress Control Number: 2016907799

Connett, J. Christian, 1973 -
Principles of Digital Marketing: 7 Keys to Online Success in Today's Information Economy. – 2nd ed.

ISBN: 978-1-5331-7887-9

Layout & Design by Connett Consulting, LLC
Editing by Andrew Schwarz\

This book can be made available at special discounts when purchased in bulk for fundraising or educational use. Special editions can also be created by request. For details, contact Forvera Media:
books@connettconsulting.com

Printed in the United States of America
First Printing June 2016
10 9 8 7 6 5 4 3 2

f o r v e r a

This book is dedicated to the people that have encouraged and pushed
me over the years never to give up, stay focused and work hard to
accomplish my dreams: My Grandmother *Vera Alice Connett*, Aunt
Connie Luffy, & my Brother *Che Connett*.

I dedicate this book to my beautiful daughters:
Kaitlynn, *Madison*, & *Savanah*.
I love you all beyond words.

PRINCIPLES OF
DIGITAL MARKETING

7 Keys to Online Success in
Today's Information Economy

CONTENTS

Foreword *by Andrew T. Schwarz, MBA*   xi

Acknowledgements   xiii

Introduction   xv

Digital Marketing Plan   1

    Digital Marketing Today   3

    Digital Marketing Plan   4

    Digital Marketing Plan Outline   8

    Hub & Spoke   14

Auditing & Scheduling   17

    Let's Conduct an Audit   19

    Channel Inventory   21

    Let's Create a Schedule   23

    Social Tools   25

    Shift Into Automatic   27

    Use This, Then That   28

    Automation Saves   30

Optimize the Channels   33

    Digital Optimization   35

    According to Google   36

    Website Optimization   37

    Social Media Optimization   39

    Marketing Optimization   40

    Another Note to Ponder   43

Content Creation & Management   47

Channel Surfing 49

Products & Services Speak 50

Manage Your Content 52

Questions to Ask Yourself 53

Reputation Intelligence & Analytics 61

Emotional Intelligence 63

Learning Intelligence 64

Channel Intelligence 65

Let Google Alert You 65

Analyzing Social 66

Google Analytics 69

Social Reports 70

Growth Hacking 75

Growth Hacker vs Marketer 77

Getting Personal 78

Listening to the Audience 79

Growing the Audience 80

Redefine Growth 81

SEO Tips & Tricks 85

SEO Legends & Myths 87

SEO You Need to Know 88

Going Mobile 90

Google Knows 90

Optimum Submission 91

Resources 101

About the Author 103

Socialize 104

FOREWORD

In today's digital economy, information can often be likened to a set of arrows placed in a quiver during a good hunt. Likewise, the information outlined in J. Christian Connett's Principles of Digital Marketing, 7 Keys to Online Success in Today's Information Economy can provide some very useful information to anyone seeking the wisdom and counsel of a well informed and technologically skilled digital marketing advisor.

The technological skills and information presented here will aid in correctly hitting the target each and every time whenever it comes to making the best use of the social media technology available today and going forward. When it comes to an ever-changing digital information economy, technology, and social media challenges can often be daunting and confusing.

The new digital landscape for social media opportunities requires the ability to adapt quickly to new and often unfamiliar territory at a moment's notice. A working knowledge of this modern arena can propel any endeavor toward success and prosperity.

Christian ultimately cares about providing his clients with the proper social media skills and information to assist anyone desiring to make the best use of these new digital opportunities available today. In the several years that I have known Christian, I have learned that the true entrepreneurial spirit runs deep in this man's veins and his passion for helping others to make the best use of the information economy will contribute to shedding some much-needed light on this topic for any information seeker.

Christian's depth of knowledge on the various subjects includes the importance of developing a digital marketing plan, conducting audits and scheduling, proper channel optimization, content creation, analytics and of course, search engine optimization. Christian has many years of experience in determining what works and what does not function so well when it relates to proper social media management and engineering.

I know this man personally, I trust his level of knowledge, and I highly recommend the information he has made available here, and wish you the best in hitting your target each and every time when using your own sharpened digital marketing arrows in your quiver of information.

Sincerely,
Andrew Tait Schwarz, MBA

ACKNOWLEDGEMENTS

This book would not be possible if it were not for all of the business owners, entrepreneurs, executives, consultants and various folks in and out of the industry that I have encountered over the years. I have consulted at many different organizations and locations. Fortunately these opportunities have helped me to learn and experience a great deal over the years.

I have had the pleasure of working with some incredible people at Norwest/Wells Fargo, TeamQuest, Bloodgood Sharp Buster, Principal Financial, Marsh & McLennan Companies / Mercer, Modular Products, Flying Hippo, Aviva, Iowa Soccer Association, and countless others.

I would like to thank the many people who have had an impact, in some way or another, on this book. I do want to name quite a few, but I cannot name everyone so if you do not see your name here, please know that I still love and appreciate you!

So, I am taking a moment to thank the following people for the love, support, inspiration, ideas, determination, reminders, drive, pushing, encouraging, and putting up with my eccentric madness:

ACKNOWLEDGEMENTS

Mariah Andreasen, Monte Ballard, Steve Bendy, Joe Brammer, Carl Burnett, Hunter Cain, Suezet Cain, Eric Carlson, Che Connett, Cheyenne Connett, Rhonda Connett, Peter Constant, Steven Ekanger, Ralph Waldo Emerson, Phil Gerbyshak, Seth Godin, Kelly Godwin, Tas Gopinath, Traci Grant, Lisa Greenwood, Eric Groves, Jon Groves, Jeff Gullion, Jaque Harmon, Jeanette Harris, Claudia Hudson, Steve Hudspeth, Igor Khalandovskiy, Laura Kinnard, Ann Kolsrud, Kevin Krefting, Abraham Lincoln, Martin Lucas, Michelle Ludt, Jules Marcoux, Jackie Monzon, Damon Moreno, Thor Moreno, Heidi Myers, Michael Neubauer, Heather Oberender, Jenny O'Dell (Fugate), Ryan Parlee, Christine Parmerlee, Patrick Perkins, Randi Pruitt, Sreenu Raju, Win Reither, Kathleen Riessen, Phil Ripperger, Jim Rohn, Silvica Rosca, Johanna Rothman, Lucas Sampson, Mike Sansone, Taylor Shore, James-Simon Schmidt, Andrew T. Schwarz, Larissa Schwartz, Chris Sinclair, Jenny St John, Kati Stout, Brett Trout, Ryan Twedt, Gary Vaynerchuk, Holli Whitacre, Chris Widener, Eric Wildman, Jenny Wood, Greg & Susan Wright, and of course my Mother, Father and God for giving me breath.

This book is in remembrance of precious loved ones that have come and gone, but are still loved and missed:

Vera A. Connett
Mary Moreno
Ashley R. Dutcher

INTRODUCTION

Do you find yourself confused and maybe even frustrated by the Internet and all these damn clichés, catchphrases and ways of *"creating money while you sleep"* promises?

In this book, I will share with you what I believe are seven (7) keys to developing your own Digital Marketing Strategy that will help you reach your target audiences in ways that matter and ways that make sense. You don't need to pay an agency or professional consultant to do everything for you.

I wrote this book because I have been teaching SMB's how to leverage Digital Marketing for years, and I know how exasperating it can be to feel like you have to spend an endless amount of your hard-earned cash to have so-called specialists and gurus do the work that you can do yourself. With a little research and effort, it will pay-off in the end.

Each Chapter of the 7 Keys, gives you a no-nonsense "how-to" blueprint for your Digital Marketing efforts that will help you achieve results that are meaningful. I want to share with you an easy-to-use guide for online success.

This book came about for many reasons, and one of which was a life-changing event that triggered my determination to make this happen. I have spent many years on the web, falling in love with information architecture, marketing, and social media.

This book is a long time in the making. I have started many times over and over. I have written white papers, blog posts, and even sketched out note after note. However, I had become discouraged along the way because I felt like every time that I started to write, something would change. The Internet is an ever-changing and fluctuating beast. Things change from month to month and day to day. It's never the same.

I purchased a Trademark back in 2008 for my white paper – Taking your business from brick and mortar to click and order®. I truly intended to turn that into a book, but it never came to fruition. I have spent years consulting with companies of all sizes from small Ma & Pa shops to Fortune 500 companies, developing strategies, websites, search engine optimization, social media marketing, etc. From 1998 to 2014 I would do all of these crazy marketing and strategy tactics to create and grow online businesses. I was in love with what I was doing, and it felt like passion more than work.

As life struggles happened, I had difficulty keeping that passion and fire alive. I was frustrated with many things in the industry, including the fact that small businesses were paying through the nose for SEO and Web development. As I was teaching my students in their college class for Interactive Media, I realized that I loved telling them how to do what these professional agencies charged a lot of money to accomplish. Some of them listened, some of them learned, and hopefully some of them apply it.

I decided I wanted to find a way to start teaching SMB's how to do these things themselves, and I began speaking at seminars and workshops teaching these business owners how to make their digital marketing efforts more successful. Many SMB's do not want to spend $300 per month on ad campaigns or ongoing search engine optimization, when much of this can be done organically and by the organization owners themselves. You have this book in your hand because you have an interest in learning about Digital Marketing and hopefully have the drive to follow through the book, create your Digital Marketing Plan and Strategy, and start forging your online success.

The purpose of this book is to help you create a reasonable, and results-oriented Digital Marketing Plan. I wanted to speak in plain English, not overuse fancy or confusing jargon or catch-phrases. I try to simplify solutions and outline the steps for a meaningful strategy.

This book is not intended to be an in-depth, innovative guide to Digital Marketing for professionals to advance their careers. Although I do think that everyone can take something from the information in this book, it is intended as a sort of beginner's guide to digital marketing. Some of the methods outlined in this book are a little more complex, but everything is feasible with a little effort and work.

I welcome your feedback and thoughts, and I truly hope that you can absorb some useful and significant digital marketing insights from this book.

"Life happens no matter what, and we must embrace it as it comes. Always remember that life is perception and that every day is a new day."
~ Christian Connett

1

DIGITAL MARKETING PLAN

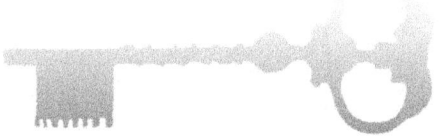

1

D igital Marketing has become the catchphrase of the last couple of years describing how you market online. This list comprises search engines, social media, blogs, and a plethora of platforms dedicated to delivering content. Content that will be accessible via an array of digital appliances that include desktop computers, phones, and tablets. When I first started my foray into the World Wide Web back in 1998, we were called "webmasters" and "new media specialists." There have been, and still are, many terms that have been used over the years to describe what is inherently an Internet marketer.

Digital Marketing Today

Today, Digital Marketing covers the gambit of Internet marketing, mobile advertising, and social media mayhem that we've all come to love and cherish. Digital Marketing can aid in driving customers and promoting your business online. My interest-turned-passion for the Internet began early on in my career, (*remember I started back in 1998*) when I developed a multi-million-dollar business listing/profile website called ShopNLocal. The site launched in early 2000.

ShopNLocal fundamentally provided small businesses a way to get onto the web by providing them with a business page listing on our extensive website. It was divided up by State and City, and then by specialty (*e.g. Plumbers, Electricians, Restaurants, Automotive, etc.*). We essentially provided what Facebook now calls "business pages."

Unfortunately, it didn't take long for competitors to swarm in and buy us out, and then abruptly dissolved the site to eliminate the competition. What I learned from ShopNLocal is what it took to make the site profitable and the individual business pages' function for the visitor, not just the business owners themselves. The client visiting your site or page or profile is ultimately your primary target. It doesn't matter if you think you've got the next million-dollar idea or website that wins awards because *YOU* like it; it matters if your *VISITORS* like it and want to come back.

Digital Marketing Plan

The purpose of this book is to give you an outline and blueprint for producing essential Digital Marketing ingredients and getting the most out of those efforts that you spend your time on, and that was hard-earned. I assume that you already have some basic knowledge of websites, social media and maybe even have your individual idea of what the definition of Digital Marketing is. I implore you to dive into this workbook and experience each chapter and the enclosed elements and principles as a plan and outline of how to get the most out of your Digital Marketing endeavors.

Creating your Digital Marketing plan should be one of the first things you do, right now, before you do anything else. It doesn't matter if you have all of your social media channels already setup, Google has indexed your site, and you've been online for ten (10) years. It is never too late to start over, which is precisely what I want you to do. Start over, right now, after all, you have already taken the first step with this book in your hands.

Some things to keep in mind when creating your Digital Marketing Plan. The first thing is to identify your target audience. Who visits your website? Who follows you on Social Media? Who does the most business with you? What market or industry do you place your focus? Answering these questions will help you begin to identify your current customers and potential prospects. You can research your industry or competitors to get an idea of your targets. Competitor analysis is always a helpful indicator, just make sure you're analyzing the most successful competitor or commensurate organization in your relevant industry.

One of the most important, yet often overlooked or misunderstood components of any marketing plan is your *unique selling point*. What makes you stand out from your competitors? What makes you the *best* business or organization that your potential customers want to do business with you? Why are you unique and more superior than any of your competitors? Once you have this major piece of the puzzle, you can begin to visualize the blueprint for your specialized Digital Marketing strategy.

Your digital marketing game plan should start with you thinking of your customers first. Your plan should be customer-centric, and not just focused on your products or services. Your plan will no doubt change and evolve over time, so don't worry about making it absolutely perfect straight out of the gate. This plan is an outline for your efforts and nothing will be set in stone. Not to mention that by the time you've perfected your incredible strategy, the Internet will have changed and grown to where you will have to make adjustments, so keep in mind that your plan is flexible and dynamic, not static.

The saying goes, Keep It Simple. Define what you want to accomplish, and then outline a few realistic goals. These could be one-time goals, or these could likewise be long-term, over a period, milestones for you to accomplish the desired results. Either way, don't overwhelm yourself with too many details. One of the places you can start is by looking at your existing strategy, that is – if one exists. Whether you have a defined tactic, a mental outline, or something that is ad-hoc or just thrown together, you can look at what has worked and what has not worked. Look into what is currently working, and what areas it wouldn't hurt to improve.

Make notes of what has worked for you in the past. Measure the results and be honest with yourself about them. Keep your overall goals in mind while you look at previous achievements or attempts. You will want to make sure to note what channels seem to function the best for your organization or products or services. Focus on those channels at first, and then look for correlated channels to add to your strategy.

Once you finish this book, you may want to come back to this chapter and create your Digital Marketing Plan using the outline that I have created for you. The next few sections will help you get started. Remember to envision your plan as a dynamic and scalable framework for your marketing efforts and campaigns, because it is something that can and will always change and fluctuate according to your specific needs.

As with any Marketing plan, you will want measurable results to determine the success of your campaign, or you will be wasting your time, right? So determine now, what is it that you want to accomplish by launching a Digital Marketing campaign? Now write that down. Write it in pencil, because you might decide you need to change some things later to fit the campaign better. It's a good process to keep activities as individual entities because each campaign may require a different perspective and different channels to be successful.

It might seem old-school actually to write things down, so if you feel better typing it out, go ahead and use your favorite text editor, or email app and type out some goals. You can always use a whiteboard and sticky notes. That process has helped me on multiple occasions especially when working with a room full of various thinkers and project sponsors that all have varied ideas of what needs to be addressed.

Remember to be realistic; thinking that you'll have 1000 all new customers in 30 days is probably a stretch unless of course your budget allows. Give yourself, and your campaign, time to grow and evolve into achieving your goals. I will talk more about analytics and tracking your results later.

I always like to point out to clients that it can take a few days to see any real results from the launch of a new campaign. The web is also a massively competitive arena. However, the more unique your product or service, the better your results are going to be. The more competition for your goods and / or services, the more unique your campaign needs to be.

Think outside of the box, and what will gain the attention and admiration of prospective customers. It isn't just all about what you want; it is all about what your client wants. The more insight you have into your customers, the more of an edge you will have for your plan of action.

Digital Marketing Plan Outline

This Digital Marketing Plan Outline is intended to help you create a strategy that will get you fast-tracked into your online campaigns. For the purpose of this plan outline, I am utilizing the SMART methodology, also referred to as SMART criteria. SMART is a mnemonic acronym, and it commonly used in Project Management.

The principal advantage of **SMART** objectives is that they are easier to understand and to know when they have been done.

Specific – target a specific area for improvement.

Measurable – quantify or suggest an indicator of progress.

Assignable – specify who will do it.

Realistic – state what results can realistically be achieved, given available resources.

Time-related – specify when the result(s) can be achieved.

Excerpts from wikipedia.org SMART_criteria

Creating your Digital Marketing Plan starts with a simple outline. The process should go quickly, by starting with a few ideas that you jot down. Go old-school and chunk out some ideas on paper. Remember, these are just ideas to outline, and you can return later and expand on them as you think of more details.

1.) Create an outline to target your budget and the ultimate goals that you want to reach. The Plan is an integral part of your agenda.

Budget:

_____

Goals: _____

_____

_____

Example goals: grow individual channel following, increase website traffic, grow an email list, better search engine results, sell products or services, brand affinity, etc.

You will want to decide on two or three solid goals that are relevant to you and your brand. Try to prioritize them because it will help you to think in terms of importance.

Goals should always be realistic and ultimately important to your overall business goals. If you want to increase your bottom line, which I assume is your purpose, then you want to create goals that will achieve that growth. You may need to focus on a more specific goal, such as brand affinity, which will build and help to grow your revenue stream.

2.) Decide how you will measure progress during a campaign.

How will you measure the success of your goals? _____

_____

_____

_____

Quantifying your outcomes will help you to hold yourself accountable for reaching the goals you are creating. This will help you to have a clear indication of success or the need for additional focus on a particular goal or area. 10% - 20% growth is a realistic benchmark for measuring results.

Your objectives can always be broken up into smaller milestones to help you reach the individual goals you are hoping to attain. By breaking these up into more manageable indicators, you may be better able to measure your journey toward the success of your goals.

3.) Elect the persons who will perform the actions that are needed to accomplish your desired goals.

Who will help to reach your goals (or will it be handled by you specifically):

_____

_____

Sharing your goals and objectives with the individuals helping you is important for a couple of reasons.

Number 1)
You want them to understand the path you are attempting. This helps them to understand the vision you may have.

Number 2)
You never know what ideas may surface from having additional assistance, not to mention experience levels. Remember that when it comes to the web, users range from beginner to advanced and everywhere in between.

You will have a chance to assign personnel to individual channels in the Auditing & Scheduling chapter.

4.) Write out reasonable results that you want to achieve, with the resources that you have available. These should be relevant and goals that matter to you or your business.

Using the goals you have outlined, sketch out some realistic results.

Does this seem worthwhile? _____

Is this the right time? _____

Does this match our other efforts/needs? _____

Do you have the right personnel? _____

Relevant goals (when met) drive the team, department, and organization forward. A goal that supports or is in alignment with other goals would be considered a relevant goal.[1]

----

[1] *Excerpt from Wikipedia.org*

5.) Determine a realistic timeline that you would like to achieve your goals. If needed, break out a journey for your milestones. Your timeframe could be a week, a month, or even a year.

What is the overall timeframe: _____

_____

What can be done now: _____

_____

What can be done halfway through?: _____

_____

What can be done prior to launch?: _____

_____

Setting time-bound goals or milestones will help to establish a sense of urgency and prevent goals from being overtaken by the day-to-day crises that invariably arise in every project.

Hub & Spoke

I utilize a methodology that I call, the *Hub & Spoke*. I have employed this method for many years, and it has helped several businesses focus and manage their objectives.

The Hub is your overall starting point, as well as the endpoint of all of your actions moving forward. The Hub is where you where you will ultimately want visitors to end up. This could be one of your Social channels, or this could be your primary website. You want them to view your products or services, and you want them to contact you and do business with you.

The Spokes are the individual channels and sites that bring visitors to your Hub. Social channels, blogs, search engines, and other websites are the Spokes that you want to capitalize on for your Digital Marketing Plan.

As of the writing of this book, I have been utilizing the following Social channels for my marketing efforts: Facebook, Twitter, Pinterest, Instagram, SnapChat, Tumblr and Anchor (*in no particular order*). By no means is this list an exhaustive list of networks, this is just a list of what I personally use and have experience with. I use my primary website, ChristianConnett.com, and Twitter to promote my content curation. You don't *have* to use your website as your Hub, you can make any one of your Social channels as your endpoint, just be sure that you have a call-to-action wherever you decide to make your Hub.

Notes & Takeaways

Notes & Takeaways

2

AUDITING & SCHEDULING

One of the most difficult things to decide on, aside from *what* to post, is *when* to post and how often. Various thoughts and methodologies seem to surround these questions, but eventually, you will discover what works best for you. To start out you can create a simple schedule, maybe only post twice a week. Later on, you can change that to post more frequently or less frequently. You just need to start.

There are many great tools to help you manage and schedule your posts. But I would like to help you outline your particular process before you start utilizing all of the available apps out there. The apps and services available are plentiful, but you should justly understand the nature of scheduling and auditing your posts and goals respectively before you dive into posting with blind abandon.

Let's Conduct an Audit

One of the first things you will want to do, especially if you've already been posting content on your site and Social channels, is to conduct an audit. It's not all daunting and scary like and IRS audit. A channel audit is a relatively simple process to determine your current goals, alignment, and what is working and what is not working.

You will want to create a spreadsheet or something easy for you to manage and edit. For the purposes of this book, I am going to be referring to a spreadsheet.

You will want to create four columns for your Audit (*you can add more, these are just the suggested primary columns*).

1) **Channel** – What are each of your networks/sites?

    Keep track of all of the networks and channels where you or your business are represented.

2) **URL** – What is the respective URL to the channel?

    Keep track of all of your usernames or URLs for all of your sites and channels.

3) **Branded** – Has each channel been branded consistently?

    Make sure that each channel/network is branded and has the same consistent look and feel, as much as the particular website will allow.

4) **Frequency** – How often do you want to update this channel?

    Decide on a frequency timeframe for each channel that makes the most sense; daily, weekly, monthly, etc. If you want to update all channels at the same time, then note that.

Take a few moments and gather your channels, URLs, etc. and add them to the worksheet on the next page. You can always make a copy of the page if it's easier than writing in the book.

Channel Inventory

CHANNEL	URL	B?	F
Facebook	/JChristianConnett	Y	D
Facebook			
Twitter			
Instagram			
Pinterest			
YouTube			
Tumblr			
SnapChat			

Take some time and examine each of your channels, ensuring that you know where each of your channels are. If you need to, Google your business or organization to find others you may have missed, and create new ones as needed. You will want to make sure that you have a direct link to your channel. Making sure that each channel has been branded accurately is very important for consistency and presentation.

Last, but not least – how frequent, or infrequent, do you want to post to this particular channel? My recommendation would be that you post to each channel at a minimum of once per month, even a simple update.

It is a good idea to take some time and go through a few Google searches. Maybe add a column to your audit to track where you fall in Google results for each respective channel. For instance, when I Google "Christian Connett": my primary website is the number 1 result, followed by Twitter at #2, LinkedIn at #3, Facebook at #4, and so on.

I have been consistent at making sure that my personal brand is spelled correctly, my title – "Digital Marketing Architect" is used throughout, and that my channels are optimized accordingly.

It may also be a good idea to add a few additional columns to your Audit sheet, especially if you have more than one person managing channels. It is not a bad idea to keep track of each channels username (*which is hopefully somewhat consistent across your channels*), as well as the individual passwords for each account (*optional*). Depending on how many personnel will be managing your channels, it may be a good idea to add a column for personnel.

The reason I feel that the Audit is so important is that it becomes a valuable management asset for your channels so that you don't forget to post to one of them, and so that you utilize each one. Remember, these channels are your spokes that bring visitors to your primary hub, so you want to have every representation that you can. It is possible to 'own' the entire first page of a search engine for your brand. It just takes a little patience, work, and time.

Now that you have your Audit completed, it's time to start thinking about what channels are the most important. If you would like to take a moment to prioritize and move some things around, now is a good time. You can continue using this spreadsheet as the basis or starting point for your schedule sheet.

You may want to take a quick moment to establish a scenario for adding channels in the future. Leave room for developing additional channels that will become available at a later date, or one that you've decided to start harnessing and utilizing.

Let's Create a Schedule

Create another spreadsheet with multiple columns to manage your posting schedule and the respective channels where you'd like to post your content. Columns should include Channel, Article Title, and Post Date. This plan becomes your content or editorial calendar and a great reference when you're not sure what is about to be posted, or what can be moved around for more imperative information.

The idea of scheduling isn't just so you can plan what to post and when. It is also so that you can create a dynamic and easy-to-use roadmap for your content. Eventually, you will develop a habit or pattern with your posting techniques and timing. This basic schedule outline is an excellent way to keep track of the content you're going to post, when you are going to post it, and what channels you will post on.

You will want to make copies of your sheet for each posting cycle. For instance, if you're going to post monthly, create a new calendar sheet for each month. Simply name them for each corresponding month (e.g. 2016-Schedule-June). The calendars will help you to organize and keep track of what you *are* going to post, as well as what you *have* posted. This will be especially important if multiple people handle the tasks of posting to your channels.

You don't need to start thinking ahead over the next 12 months about what you are going to be posting. The calendar is so that you can add items as you move forward. If you have ideas for upcoming posts or articles, then by all means add titles or notes for what you'd like to write and what channels will be included in a list.

I like to specify the topic, title, and a description for each post on the calendar. Add a column for each channel and then check off each with an 'X', or add a date to each matching column to specify if the post will be applied to that channel.

One of the beauties of online culture is the fact that there are many resources for creating & storing your schedules online.

Social Tools

There are some prodigious tools and services available on the web for scheduling and managing social media posts. Some offer free versions or options; some offer premium services for a premium price – monthly or annually. I won't cover all the tools out there, just the ones that I am familiar enough with and that I have found success utilizing. It's imperative that you determine what channels are the most important for you to manage.

Buffer – *j2c.me/JC-Buffer* - Buffer helps you to schedule and shares your content at the best possible times throughout the day so that your followers and fans see your updates more often. Get the most out of each post. As you add content, you can easily select which of your social accounts you want to post to. Post the same message to all accounts or add context by customizing each.

Create images with the perfect size and format for Twitter, Facebook, Instagram, and even Pinterest using Buffer App - **Pablo**. Typography, font sizes, and formatting options make everyone a designer! Whether you are browsing the web or on the go, you can easily add content to your queue with the Buffer browser extensions and mobile apps. Save time and get more done by working from anywhere. [2]

Hootsuite - *j2c.me/JC-Hootsuite* is another great tool for managing multiple accounts at once (*up to 50 with one of their premium accounts*) and multiple users. The free version of Hootsuite will allow you to manage up to 3 Social accounts at once. They provide analytics and basic message scheduling. You can schedule out your posts and manage your profiles, mentions, timelines, etc. Hootsuite provides a simple interface for posting across multiple channels with characters counts and an easy to use scheduling tool. There are several other options available in Hootsuite that are beyond the scope of this book.

Later - *j2c.me/IG-Later* "The simpler way to plan your visual content marketing". Later helps you plan, manage, and schedule your visual social media posts and marketing campaigns for Instagram. Save time scheduling and managing your Instagram posts with the visual calendar. The calendar allows you to create and upload image posts on desktop or the mobile app to be posted at a later date. You could potentially plan the next week of posts or more. The free account allows 30 posts per month and two social profiles. Use my referral link above and get an extra 10 posts.

---

[2] *Excerpts from buffer.com*

Later has some great Instagram features that include: Search and repost, preview posts prior to posting, as well as mobile app & desktop management. Later offers a FREE account, which is probably enough to get you up and running for a few months until your needs grow. They offer three other paid accounts that each add-on more features. Check out their comparisons to decide what plan works best for you.

If you are primarily focusing on **Facebook**, then you should utilize the **Facebook Business Manager**. If you are not familiar with the FBM, I recommend you take a look here: ***j2c.me/FB-BusinessManager***. It allows you to manage your Facebook ad accounts, Pages, apps and the people who work on them — all in one place, and it's FREE.[3]

Shift into Automatic

Something that has been a tremendous powerhouse for my business process as well as my clients is streamlining online marketing efforts. Automation is a favorite method of marketing in my arsenal. The ability to post once and broadcast your message across multiple channels will not only save you time and effort, but it will also ensure that your message is consistent across your networks.

Logging into each of your networks and copying and pasting your content over and over again can not only be time-consuming, but it can indeed create the probability for inconsistencies and open yourself up to errors, or forgetting a valuable channel. Wouldn't it be easier and more

---

[3] *Excerpt from facebook.com*

helpful if you could publish your content once and have it posted out to each and every channel that you choose?

So, how do we shift into automatic? It can start with your website, or it can start with any one of your Social channels. If you have not heard of **IFTTT** aka "If This, Then That" - *j2c.me/JC-IFTTT*, then you are missing out on an extremely valuable and FREE tool for many aspects of your business and your life overall. IFTTT is an automation service that connects with numerous accounts across several mediums including social media, websites, smart home appliances, Android, iOS, and much, much more.

Use This, Then That

IFTTT can help you automate your business and life in many ways. Connect with over 300 services that include automating parts of your home, keeping in touch with friends and family, being more productive in life and business, get news and weather alerts and updates automatically delivered to your phone, connect your health apps, shop smarter, and so much more.

For the purpose of this book, I will focus on using IFTTT for marketing automation. I implore you to visit IFTTT and look into their service more in-depth. The best part... it is a FREE service without any limitations. iOS and Android apps are available, as well as a "DO", "DO note", and "DO camera" apps for extending their service offerings.

IFTTT will allow you to do simple, complex, and some very surprising things as well. You can access their website from your desktop (*or mobile*) and then install the app on your mobile device and utilize many of the connected services directly from your device. You essentially create recipes. These recipes are connecting one service to another service to automate an event or multiple events. Many of these recipes can be edited and managed by location, time, or even action specific.

For instance, you can connect your Facebook (*either personal or business page*) and then connect your Twitter account to IFTTT. Then just create a recipe that will update your Twitter profile picture with your Facebook profile picture each time you update it. This particular scenario can also work in the reverse.

You can connect your Instagram account, create an image post, and then automatically post a Tweet that includes your image and any caption as a post. You can simultaneously post the image and caption to your Tumblr site, Facebook, and respectively pin to a board on Pinterest, etc. With IFTTT you can automate your posts from just about any network to most any other network simultaneously.

You can power your business automating more than just Social media. Sync and back up your contacts; save content into your Evernote notebooks; monitor the competition; save photos from many of your online accounts; control your Wi-Fi; monitor your home or vehicles, manage critical tasks & notifications; automate your email, calendars, and the list goes on. IFTTT has a tremendous amount of possibilities and recipes associated with their service.

If you use a Content Management System (CMS) for your website, then you may also have plugins or modules available that can automate and integrate IFTTT with many of these processes for you. Using these plugins and modules coupled with IFTTT, the automation possibilities are endless. Joomla and Drupal have modules available for auto posting. WordPress has become my preferred de facto CMS, combined with a collection of preferred plugins for auto-posting and updating.

Everyone has a different need when it comes to automation. One of the many avenues of Content Marketing that I engage in, is curating beneficial marketing content, from multiple sources and then share out via Twitter, LinkedIn, Tumblr and Facebook. I automate my Instagram posts to share out to my social channels, including pinning the images and captions to a Pinterest board.

Automation Saves

Employing IFTTT and automation, in general, has saved me thousands of hours over the last couple of years, and their platform continues to improve features and services that can help you manage a great deal of your business and personal life.

Streamlining your efforts with automation will make certain that your messages are consistent across the web, and minimize time constraints. Look for other ways to automate and streamline your marketing and content dissemination that will free up time to do other things, like offline marketing – aka – running your business that you're promoting.

Notes & Takeaways

_____

_____

_____

_____

_____

_____

_____

_____

_____

_____

_____

_____

Notes & Takeaways

_____

_____

_____

_____

_____

_____

_____

_____

_____

_____

_____

_____

3

OPTIMIZE THE CHANNELS

A vital step in a successful digital marketing strategy is to ensure that you have optimized all of your profiles. These profiles include each Social Media channel, website, video outlet, and any online property that carries a representation of you or your organization. These should all be perceived as valuable real estate.

I should not need to stress the importance of appearance, but as the adage goes - you do not get a second chance at a first impression, especially on the web. If you aren't reaching your visitor or audience the moment they reach your page, post or image – you may lose an opportunity to capture their affinity and most likely, a prospect and the worst loss of all, a sale.

Digital Optimization

The definition of optimizing is to make the best or most efficient use of your resources to improve the efficiency and outcome of your efforts. Just to be clear, the object of digital optimizing is making sure that all of your online real estate (*e.g. websites, profiles, etc.*) have a consistent use of appropriate graphics and content, and that they are constant across all channels.

Be sure that each of your websites and all of your social media accounts have a representative icon, picture or graphic that catches the eye of your visitors.

Your primary icon or image should be something that is an appropriate depiction of you or your organization, and something that is indicative of the content the viewer is about to encounter. Think of McDonald's or Ford, they both have iconic brand images, logos, and graphics that are recognizable across all mediums.

According to Google

In the USA, 94% of people with smartphones search for local information on their phones. Interestingly, 77% of mobile searches occur at home or at work, places where desktop computers are likely to be present. Mobile is critical to your business and will continue to be so – whether you're blogging about your favorite sports team, working on the website for your community theater, or selling products to potential clients. Make sure visitors can have a good experience on your site when they're visiting from their mobile devices! [4]

Have you ever tapped on a Google Search result on your mobile phone, only to find yourself looking at a page where the text was too small, the links were tiny, and you had to scroll sideways to see all the content? This usually happens when the website has not been optimized

---

[4] *Excerpt from developers.google.com/webmasters/mobile-sites/#why*

to be viewed on a mobile phone. [5] All of the major search engines have one thing in common: to make money from their business of search. You cannot forget that when you're planning and promoting your content. The search engines are a major key to your online survival, and potentially a jumping point for web traffic.

Website Optimization

The major concentration of all optimization is your website. Take care that your website gets optimized in every aspect, and not just Search Engine Optimization (*which will be covered later in this book*).

I want to stress the importance of Responsive Web Design. Your website needs to be responsive to the plethora of devices that are accessing it. Whether on a desktop, or mobile device, you will want to make sure that your visitors can view your website content however, they feel comfortable accessing your site. Your visitors are using Phones, tablets, and desktop monitors of all shapes and sizes.

The other factor is that Google along with the other search engines will not show your site any favor in results if it is not what they deem "mobile-friendly".

---

[5] *Excerpt from webmasters.googleblog.com/2014/11/helping-users-find-mobile-friendly-pages.html*

Website optimization includes using the proper navigation to get your visitors where they want to be within 2-3 clicks, or you absolutely risk losing your prospects. Content placement on each page is important so that the site visitor can determine if they want to purchase your products or services, and of course, you should always feature prominent links to all of your social media channels.

Your primary website is where you want to make sure that you are not just linking to your channels, but that you have included the respective icons, direct links, and proper alt and title text in your HTML.

Something that you should establish on each page of your website, and each post, especially if you are planning to link to a specific page; is adding a relevant image to the top of each post/page. A well-chosen image is not only attention grabbing for the visitor and reader, but it is also utilized for the social channel which will extract that graphic and use it as the primary image or header for your URL to the respective page on your site or in your blog. You should always use images that are symbolic and content-relevant so that your visitors are never confused about what they are viewing.

Remember that not all visits will be to the home page of your website. Oftentimes you will want to link to more internal pages, or blog posts of your website rather than just the home page. This deep-linking can be crucial for drawing your prospects in, as well as leading your visitors directly to a specific product or article that you are promoting via your channels. This helps to get your visitor directly to the resource of information that they are seeking and better the odds of gaining attraction and a prospective client.

Social Media Optimization

The other critical component of optimizing will be enhancing all of your social media channels. This is where it is important to make sure that all profiles have emblematic images and graphics, as well as a header image (*where applicable*) sometimes called a cover image. These should always be something that is demonstrative of your organization and what you are representing.

Optimizing your website and social channels are important steps for branding and creating affinity, which is something that is very critical for you and the organization you symbolize. Whether it's a company branding that you're displaying or your personal brand, you need to make sure that all of your channels show the same consistent look and feel. This will ensure that your visitors are not confused when they visit your different channels and that they know that they are visiting the same organization no matter what channel they have arrived at.

You should formulate 2 to 3 short sentences that describe your primary business or organization. This is something that can be used across all of your channels and will help to keep your brand message consistent. Some channels only allow a certain number of characters (*e.g. Twitter or Instagram*), while other channels allow a greater number of characters to be used. Be sure that when you use descriptions in your profiles, that you take advantage of any additional features that each individual channel offers.

Instagram and SnapChat are great platforms to utilize one or two emoji's in your bio or username, respectively. Instagram is image-based, so the use of emoji is acceptable, just don't over-do-it with silly emoji's that have little to do with what your description says or what you exemplify. SnapChat is a good place to use an emoji at the *end* of your username, for attention grabbing purposes. Remember that if you use an emoji at the beginning of your SnapChat username, your name will show toward the bottom of your followers & friends list (*symbols and emoji's get last result listing*).

Instagram limits your bio to 150 characters, so use those characters, including whitespace and emoji, intelligently. Check the desktop version of your profile as well at *instagram.com/yourusername*. Your Bio text will appear as you want it formatted on mobile, but will appear collapsed on a desktop.

Marketing Optimization

An excellent way to utilize the Instagram URL field is to link directly to your blog, or a particular product or service page. This doesn't have to be stagnant. Change the URL frequently to reflect your current marketing or campaign efforts. Create an image post that references what the visitor might find by "clicking the URL in the bio". You can change this URL frequently to match image posts in the future. This creates a unique opportunity to keep your profile fresh and changing often.

Facebook has a couple of unique ways that you can optimize your profile. Whether utilizing a personal or business page, the profile image appears across all of your posts and in the News Feed. Make sure it's iconic in nature and relevant to your overall profile. Use the cover image to immediately catch the eye of your visitor.

Facebook's Cover Guidelines state: "For your Page's cover photo, use a unique image that represents your Page. This might be a photo of a popular menu item, album artwork or a picture of people using your product. Be creative and experiment with images to see what your audience responds to best."

Facebook provides help resources for your business page here: *j2c.me/FB-PagesHelp*

The primary areas to focus on for your Facebook page, is your profile image and the cover image, as they are the first spaces that someone sees when accessing your page. The other thing to focus on, is your individual posts themselves. Remember to always use a primary image if you are posting directly onto your Timeline. Add an image, create a title and then the description to your post. Make your post clean and easy to read, use bullet points if you can (*they are easier to read at a glance*). Where possible, add a link in the post, hopefully linking out to your primary hub.

There are two ways to manage the content on your business page. The first way to bring customers to your website from the channel is to post excerpts of the pages or posts from your website by placing truncated content into your Facebook post, then pasting the page/post URL into the bottom of your post content. This should provide you with a preview of the image that Facebook pulls in from your site, hopefully, your intended featured image for the respective page or post. It is proven that posts with pictures and links garner more engagement than just a simple text-oriented post.

The second way of sharing content is when you are planning on utilizing videos in your posts. Facebook will give more favor to native uploads than a link out to another service, or a YouTube or Vimeo video embed. Where possible, you will want to upload your video to your actual Facebook post, adding an excerpt of text that perhaps describes the video content, then add a URL just below the content that will bring the viewer to your corresponding page.

It is important to always include a URL, even if you're only sharing a Twitter post, or an Instagram image on your Facebook timelines - include the full URL, as this will lead your visitor over to your other account, and eventually to your website, thus the Hub & Spoke while creating affinity.

Optimize your Twitter profile by making great use of #hashtags in your description text, as these will help your profile show up in search results for the respective tags you might utilize (*e.g. My background includes #marketing and #advertising, etc.*). Don't forget that Twitter feeds are often shown in Google results for contextually relevant searches.

You should think about what imagery can be used across other social channels as well. Twitter, Facebook, and LinkedIn all allow cover images. You will want to Google the exact specs and sizes needed for each cover, as they all differ somewhat from one another.

Be sure to pay attention to the fact that most viewers are now on mobile devices, be it phones or tablets, so when designing your cover images, research the key section or area of the image that will show best on mobile and focus on that aspect of your design. If you are hiring a graphic designer, be sure that they have vast experience designing for social media AND mobile devices.

Another Note to Ponder

Keep in mind that you do not need to use your business name, unless it is part of your marketing strategy. Most people aren't searching for *ACME Company*; they are most likely searching for *Super-Secret Sauce for chicken* from the ACME Company. You are optimizing for what your audience are seeking. Keep that in mind. Research your top competitors or others that are successful in your industry.

Notes & Takeaways

Notes & Takeaways

_____

_____

_____

_____

_____

_____

_____

_____

_____

_____

_____

_____

4

CONTENT CREATION
& MANAGEMENT

I t is easy to feel overwhelmed about creating content for your website or social media accounts. What to write about, what to post, what to share, how often, etc. But creating content is different for each business and individual.

If your website has a blog or a place where you make any news updates or posts, then that is somewhere that you can start with for content for your social media campaigns. This is where you will want to craft your post on your website, as your hub, and then share that content across your social channels.

Channel Surfing

Part of your strategy will be determining what channels to broadcast on. Sometimes it's easiest to blanket-broadcast across channels with the same message and the same content, however, other times you may want specific content strategically posted to say LinkedIn if it's more professional networking oriented. You may want to post more business-audience content on your Facebook business page, and a more concise version of that post on Twitter, with a link of course to your hub post. Remember, there are automation options for doing all of this as well.

With Instagram, it will be an image post - and should be the same as the featured image from your post, with a text overlay about the article or post you are referencing.

Using SnapChat is an excellent way to add a personal touch by

speaking briefly (*you have around 10 seconds*) about why the visitor should come check out your post or site. Be sure that you create a text-overlay call to action across your Snap with an easy to understand action (*e.g. visit acmeproducts.com for more info*). You can now also create and utilize your very own custom SnapChat on-demand Geofilters.

If you have a brick and mortar business, then your custom Geofilters can also be used by your customers giving you the potential to create fun campaigns, giveaways or sweepstakes encouraging the use of the filters, which could easily create great exposure for your business. For more information on the SnapChat custom filters, go here: **_j2c.me/SC-Geofilters_**

There are some truly unique and interesting possibilities for using the SnapChat Geofilters. Create a campaign to get people in the door, then publish a custom Geofilter for that campaign and post signage encouraging patrons to post photos on their SnapChat stories utilizing your filter.

Keep in mind that you do not have to marry yourself to posting every single day, you can post once a week maybe even every two weeks but try to keep your posting somewhat consistent. I cover this more in the chapter, *Auditing & Scheduling*.

Products & Services Speak

You know your business better than anyone else. So, start out by writing around ten things that someone could discover or appreciate about

your products, services or what your environment is like. Remember, each product itself can become a post! You can choose to highlight individual menu items, products, and services by posting about them each week, each month, or even each day if you're so inclined.

A key ingredient to creating great content that matters... BE YOURSELF. Don't try to 'sell' yourself or your products. If your services are truly great, which you believe that they are, then they will essentially sell themselves. What you are doing, is simply sharing how YOU feel about the products or services, and you want to share that experience with your clients. Let your customer decide how cutting edge or new and improved that your services are. Do not talk *at* your customers, talk *to* your customers. Share with them. Appeal to them. They are just like you, human.

Content is creating and sharing information with your customers and potential prospects. The more real you are with them, the better off you will be. Pretentious, superfluous descriptions or an egocentric persona will only put off your customers. Integrity and confidence in your products and services will encourage customers to do business with you. So, be honest.

I have not always given the best customer service or delivered the best results at points in my past, but I have learned that I have to work hard to resolve the issues. Now I can focus on how to be better the next time around. You should always do this too. There are always going to be lessons learned, and I hope that you utilize each lesson as a stepping stone in your career and your life.

Your content is about how you can improve the life or need of your customer, not how you can line your pockets. It is not just about you; it is about THE CLIENT. You can have the best products, the best service, and a magnificent marketing campaign. But if you deliver with arrogance or a selfish and narrow approach, you risk losing the customers that matter the most to your business.

1000 customers one time are great, but the same customer that keeps coming back, over and over again, is one of the most valuable assets any organization could ask for. Loyalty carries the most weight. Your customers and prospects think the same way about YOU and YOUR products, YOUR services, and what YOU have to offer. So, keep that in mind and copy the ideas - no one is going to reinvent the wheel.

Manage Your Content

What kind of website platform are you using? Do you know? Who hosts your website? Where is your Domain Name registered and who is listed as the Registrant, Administrative & Billing contacts? Who updates our website? What can they tell you about the framework of your site? How is the content managed or your site?

These are all principal and edifying questions that are paramount to your online success.

If you don't know who or what built the foundation of your website, how can you build anything on top of that dependably?

Content Management is all too important not to have much of an idea about it. Many sites today are built on hosting platforms such as SquareSpace, Weebly or Wix. Some frameworks are open source for example WordPress, Drupal, or Joomla, as well as premium or enterprise CMS that include Shout, Craft, Agility, or a myriad of other available Content Management Systems.

It is important to remember that content is more than just words or getting views on your page(s) and posts. An action is your objective. Create content that creates action. Research the best times of day (or night) that you should be posting your content.

Most analytics will help you determine the best times to post your content. There is also great value in researching the popular trending times of posts. Do the research or hire a reasonably-priced Digital Marketing professional.

Questions to Ask Yourself

It is easy to conjure up marketing and promotional ideas that make you excited just to imagine how amazing they could be. You can go out and print up some incredible posters and window clings, maybe even drop some promo cards into customers bags or hand out pamphlets or handbills announcing some great things coming up.

But, without keeping your customers at the forefront of your thinking, you might very well miss out on some important steps in your marketing agenda. Put yourself in your customer's shoes (or devices for that matter). What would you want to see on a company's social media or their website?

Ask questions of some of your most valued customers. What do they think about your products and services? How do they feel when doing business with you? Get their thoughts, sentiments, and even dislikes. Swallow your pride for a moment, because these people are the lifeblood of your business.

Another bonus that looks great on your website and social as well are testimonials from your customers. Ask that they make them descriptive so that you can employ their input as respected feedback and create campaigns that make the most sense for your client base moving forward, which will attract prospects to your business.

There are undoubtedly some valuable questions that you should ask yourself before you create another failed promotion. These are just topics and questions that I frequently ask my clients when working on their website projects.

During a consultation, it is important to put you, the client, in the shoes of a customer, because ultimately that is who we are aiming at.

❖ What compels you to buy products at a hardware or home repair store?

   o Are there specific products you know that they carry? Do you have a good customer service experience with the employees or owner? Do you feel comfortable because it's small or local? These are impulses that motivate you to visit this store.

❖ Why do you shop for groceries at your favorite grocery store?

   o Is it the branding that pulls you in? The familiarity of the store layout & business practice? The custom discounts or promotions? The convenience they offer? Do you appreciate the local aspect? What makes you choose to purchase at this particular store as opposed to similar establishments?

❖ Where do you buy your clothes, and why do you buy from them?

   o Think about where and why you purchase your clothing at specific stores or locations. What is it that helps you determine that you will shop *there* for what you need? Is it the particular brands that they carry? The reasonable pricing or affordability? The cleanliness of the store?

❖ How does each of these companies, the ones that you appreciate and enjoy, market and promote their products?
  o How are they doing it? What kinds of Call-to-action do they use? Signage? Brochures or flyers of some sort? How do they promote their goods to the degree of earning your patronage?

❖ What is it that you like about their marketing?
  o If you like their marketing and promotions, what is it about them that appeals to you? Look at how they place their signs, or the verbiage used. Do they utilize Social Media? What does their website look like that you can identify with?

❖ How do you appreciate what they have to offer?
  o What kinds feelings and emotional fulfillment can you derive from these experiences? Do you continue doing business with an organization because you truly appreciate their products or services?

❖ What do you *not* like about them?
  o Are there some things or aspects that you do not appreciate or care for at any businesses that you visit? What is it that they do, or don't do that displeases you?

❖ What makes you feel irritated?

   o What is something that turns you off or just rubs you the wrong way? Have you been in an establishment and something just pissed you off to no end? Past experiences?

❖ What makes you pleased?

   o Is there anything that makes you smile, at least occasionally when visiting your favorite store(s)? What is it that they do that you feel makes you or others happy to visit? What kind of reputation do they have?

❖ What results would you expect to find while searching Google or Bing or Yahoo!?

   o Do you have any experience with searching for a local store or looking to see if your favorite has a certain product or brand in stock? Do they frequently pop up in search results? Can you easily find them, especially when typing in their name directly?

One of the theories that I have believed in and frequently expressed over the years is that sometimes you can discover more by asking what your customer *does not like*, rather than what they *do like*. That way, you know what to avoid. You have a better chance of pleasing your clients by avoiding what they dislike, then trying to find every little detail that makes them happy.

This really is an easy to understand and accomplish process. When you're speaking with a client, it's easy enough to say, "now that we've had some time to discuss your needs and desires, can you tell me what it is that you do not like?."

Another big question to ask is "What is your frustration point?". These questions can seem innocuous or insignificant. Either belief, trust me when I tell you that you will be very surprised about what you can truly learn by asking these questions.

Notes & Takeaways

Notes & Takeaways

5

REPUTATION INTELLIGENCE & ANALYTICS

I t is paramount that you manage *and* monitor when people are talking about you online and what it is that they are saying. I like to call this: Reputation Intelligence. This process can have many different names: Brand Monitoring, Alerts, or good old-fashioned listening. It is important that you are not only monitoring but also engaging with visitors to your channels.

Emotional Intelligence

There are many facets that you need to keep an eye on. These include comments, likes, mentions, clips, reviews, snaps, videos, and more. Even if you decide to log into every channel individually, one by one and check out your insights or analytics *(most provide some degree of analytics – more on that in this chapter)*, it is imperative that you know what's being said or mentioned about you and your business.

It is equally as important that you address all of the engagements. Keep in mind that not everything that is being said will be negative, but you will want to address the negatives just as importantly as the positives because these are all your potential prospects and customers, and they are primarily "marketing" for you. So be sure to treat them accordingly.

Reputation Intelligence is not some super-secret tool or a one-size-monitors-all tool; it is a series of actions, events and ongoing activity to pay attention to what is going on in the online world, pertaining to your brand. It's important to keep up with what is being said about your organization.

Learning Intelligence

There are so many different tools and apps available to monitor all of your different channels, and it's important that you do monitor and follow what is being said about you or your organization so that you can respond as diligently and appropriately as possible. The price points for these apps range from free DIY to thousands of dollars per month or year.

I highly recommend researching and choosing the best apps or services for your budget and organization as wisely as possible. You will, of course, want the most benefit for the money. Be sure that you are choosing a service that monitors all of your social channels *completely* not just mentions of your name or organization.

Remember that everything on the web now leaves a footprint. You want to track all of your footprints, no matter how clean or dirty they are. I do want to point out that if you find something negative, address it in the best way you can. Try to put yourself in the consumers' shoes, approach it as if you were the one complaining. Don't try to cover up or bury negative commentary; address it and engage in an active and constructive manner.

You can do much of the reputation monitoring on your own, or use dedicated personnel, or hire a sensibly priced consultant to handle the job for you. You know as well as I do that any sentiments, good or bad have an impact on your brand. So, why not protect it by monitoring anything and everything you can? Let's shuffle through some ideas for your individual reputation intelligence.

Channel Intelligence

There are several channels available and ready for you to add and monitor your brand. Have a look at the list below, if you aren't on one of them – take a look and see if there is a value to your business by listing on the respective site. Sometimes it's a very good idea to at least have a presence that points to your primary hub or website. Business name, address, phone, website or social links. These are all great spokes for your brand. Many of these channels can be utilized in organic search engine results.

Some of these channels include Google, LinkedIn, Twitter, Instagram, About.me, Stumbleupon, Facebook, Pinterest, SnapChat, AnchorFM, Appearoo, BrandYourself, Hubpages, Paper.li, Scoop.it, YouTube, Reddit, Flickr, Bumpzee, Quora, Blogspot, PeekYou, WordPress.com, Yahoo Answers, FourSquare, MySpace, Diigo, Soundcloud, LiveJournal, Blogmarks.net, MetaCafe, Last.fm, Photobucket, HuffingtonPost.

Let Google Alert You

Google Alerts are a free and great way to start monitoring what someone may be posting about you or your organization online. Start by visiting google.com/alerts and enter your business or organization name.

If it is more than one word, place your brand in "quotes". My alert is set up as "Christian Connett". You can edit your alert settings and manage the frequency that you will get alerts in your email. This will be a helpful start to monitoring your reputation.

Analyzing Social

Social Media Analytics are a powerful indicator of how your channels are functioning. Social Analytics give you the ability to measure, analyze, and interpret the interactions between visitors and your properties. These all-too-important analytics can uncover customer sentiment and trends across your channels. This is also part of the intelligence factor.

You will want to monitor the data from your website as well as different social sites to aid in more comprehensive digital marketing strategies. Mining your social media figures should help to determine your Key Performance Indicators (KPI's). These KPI's will have a significant impact on your hard work going forward.

You should continuously evaluate the success of your campaigns and determine what is most important to you and your organization.

Some networks provide intrinsic analytics, although they are not too obvious where to locate them. Here are a few of the big players:

Twitter Analytics   *j2c.me/TW-Analytics*

Facebook Analytics   *j2c.me/FB-Analytics*

Pinterest Analytics   *j2c.me/PIN-Analytics*

These analytics can be accessed by logging into your account and then visiting the above URL's.

My personal favorite for Instagram analytics is called **Iconosquare** - *j2c.me/IS-Analytics* - Iconosquare provides a 7 day trial to try out the service for managing your Instagram account. At the time of writing, the cost is $4.90 per month/per account.

Providing key analytics for your Instagram account, Iconosquare is an incredible way to measure and optimize your Instagram performance. Iconosquare Instagram analytics gives you the ability to Filter by date, most liked, most commented, most engaging, most loved, and most talked about ratings.

- Manage ALL your Instagram accounts from the same interface
- Add specific users and hashtags to your feed for specific content
- Choose the date range you want to get Instagram analytics from
- Discover your followers geolocation, identify your most influent followers, sort your media by engagement rate, visualize your community structure and much more!

Iconosquare helps you understand your audience, improve your performance and engage better with your community on Instagram.[6]

- Monitor your followers and growth over time
- Know who unfollows you
- Identify new and top followers
- Optimize strategy with best time to post, filter & hashtag impact
- Sort most engaging posts by engagement rate, likes or comments
- Benchmark against your competitors
- Track your hashtag(s) performance
- Get exports (.csv) and reports (daily, weekly, monthly)

While there are an innumerable amount of analytics services and apps out there, it truly is up to you to discover what works the best for your budget and organization.

I certainly have my favorites, and I also do quite a bit of digging into the native platform analytics themselves for a more precise view of the data.

---

[6] *Excerpt from Iconosquare.com*

Google Analytics

A tremendously powerful way to help monitor your website, as well as social channels, is utilizing Google Analytics (GA). Google Analytics has become an irreplaceable cornerstone for monitoring and measuring social integration.

Integrating Google Analytics will assist in measuring your marketing efforts, your website and social traffic, your visitor's behavior, and individual campaigns using custom goal URLs for tracking. Google Analytics can help to provide ROI data by setting up goals.

Sign up or log into Google Analytics here: *j2c.me/Goo-Analytics*

You will also want to look into employing Google Tag Manager to unite with your analytics. Tag Manager will help with interaction tracking, remarketing, Google AdWords and other specific tracking needs.

Access Google Tag Manager here: *j2c.me/Goo-TM*

Focus on your goals and objectives you previously outlined in your Digital Marketing Plan for setting up your tracking and ensure that your social initiatives are aligned with your strategy. Follow the S.M.A.R.T. goals you defined earlier in the book.

Create and edit goals here: *j2c.me/Goo-Goals*

Social Reports

As of this writing, there are six Social Analytics reports available in Google Analytics. Each report will help you achieve a better understanding of the results from your campaigns. Locate the Social Reports in GA under the **Reporting** tab > then **Acquisition** > in the left-side menu, and select **Social** just under Search Engine Optimization.

Here is a quick breakdown of the Google Social Reports [7]:

The **Overview** report allows you to see at a glance how much conversion value is generated from social channels.

Navigate to **Network Referrals** to see engagement metrics (*Pageviews, Avg. Session Duration, Pages/Session*) for traffic from each social network.

Navigate to **Landing Pages** to see engagement metrics (*Pageviews, Avg. Session Duration, Pages/Session*) for each URL.

The **Conversions** report allows you to quantify the value of Social.

If you have **Plugins** such as Google "+1" or Facebook "Like" buttons on your site, it's important to know which buttons are being clicked and for which content.

The Social **Users Flow** shows the initial paths that users from social networks took through your site.

Access GA Social Analytics here: *j2c.me/Goo-SA*

---

[7] *Excerpts from Google*

There are four elements that define your social impact:

Network Referrals: As your content is shared and people come to your site, it's important to understand how users from different social sources engage with your site.

Conversions: Shared content URLs become the entry points into your site, driving traffic from social sources. Measuring the conversion and monetary value of this traffic will help you understand the impact of Social on your business.

Landing Pages: People increasingly engage with, share, and discuss content on social networks. It's important to know which pages and content are being shared, where they're being shared, and how.

Social Plugins: Adding Social Plugin buttons to your site (for example, Facebook "Like" buttons) allows your users share content to social networks directly from your site. Your social plugins data shows you which content is being shared, and on which networks.

The Social Analytics reports allow you to analyze all of this information together and see the complete picture of how Social impacts your business.[8]

---

[8] *Excerpts from support.google.com/analytics/answer/1683971*

Notes & Takeaways

Notes & Takeaways

6

GROWTH HACKING

A ccording to **Wikipedia**, the definition of Growth Hacking is *"a process of rapid experimentation across a range of marketing channels to identify the most effective ways to grow a business."* The phrase "Growth Hacker" was originally coined by **Sean Ellis,** a respected entrepreneur, angel investor, and startup advisor.

Growth hacking involves a combination of being analytical, creative, and innovative to grow your customer base. My experimentation across channels has led me to discover some fruitful and thought-provoking, if not fun, ways of building an audience as well as gaining new prospects.

Growth Hacker vs. Marketer

A growth hacker is not a replacement for a marketer. A growth hacker is not better than a marketer. A growth hacker is just different than a marketer. To use the most succinct definition from Sean (Ellis)'s post, "A person whose true north is growth. Everything they do is scrutinized by its potential impact on scalable growth." [9]

---

[9] *excerpt from The Definitive Guide to Growth Hacking by Neil Patel & Bronson Taylor*

There are numerous of ways to growth hack. I would implore you to do what works best for you, or enlist a specialist to help. Either way, SEO, email marketing, social media interactions, online forums and communities, videos, etc. are all forms of growth hacking. Engage with your audience early on in your campaigns to help establish a rapport with them. This not only proves your passion and interest in your followers, but it also allows you to communicate with them and share more content that they will care about. It's a great opportunity to ask for feedback from your audience. This works like word of mouth, just on a larger scale.

Getting Personal

You can send a private message on most channels; this is an excellent way to be more personally involved with your visitors. Take a moment and reach out to thank them for their interest or liking a post. Don't hesitate to ask for their honest opinions. Be prepared that you might not like what you hear, but appreciate the candid response and build something better from there.

Now that you've got all of these social channels, websites and various outlets at your disposal, how are you going to continue to grow your audience, engage with them and continue to reach out to them? Start by focusing your growth on one channel at a time. I usually start with the most popular channel first. Now, I don't mean the most popular regarding how many people know about the particular channel. I am talking about your brand popularity. Where do YOU thrive the most? What channel seems to draw YOUR audience?

If you have 100 followers on Twitter that don't engage much, yet 500 on Instagram and 10% are liking or commenting; then I would suggest building your Instagram audience first and foremost. The reason you do this is because there is something that is already working for you on that channel. Check your current engagements, what are your visitors liking or commenting on, what posts are they sharing?

Listening to the Audience

One of the most important factors of Growth Hacking, in my opinion; is *always* responding to your visitors. When someone comments, even if it's a simple emoji, reply back to that person by commenting (*using the @ mention where applicable*) and thank them. At the very least, use an emoji as a response. I tend to use the *top hat* emoji. 🎩 It's my favorite and somewhat of a signature if you would.

When you thank your commenters and audience, it shows your engagement and that you care. It will encourage them, more often than not, to take a look at your other posts or properties. You can ask for them to visit your other properties, but keep it subtle. The idea is to entice your visitors with useful content. This encourages them to continue to become repeat visitors and hopefully prospects for your other channels.

Then, you will want to take this one step further. I will share my hacking on Instagram as an example. When I am notified that someone has liked a few of my posts, I will visit their profile as well, and like a few (*generally a minimum of 6*) of their posts. It shows that I care and have an interest in what they've posted. Not to mention it's a good way to say "thank you", and it makes them curious about this user that just liked several of their posts. This brings back around 1 in 5 users to start following my account; thus growth hacking.

I don't always follow everyone that follows me. I don't follow everyone that likes something of mine either. But they are always worth a look. They took the time to view my post and comment or like it. The least I can do is see theirs. Besides, this often leads me to discover some great connections and allows me to network with like-minded individuals. Don't get caught falling into a rabbit hole and find yourself sidetracked from what you're actually attempting to accomplish. It is very easy to do.

Growing the Audience

Focus on building and engaging your guests, just as if you were the host of a party. It is best that you align yourself or someone else, that is dedicated to the growth hacking process and growing your core audience. It can be a part of content marketing, but it is not the same as producing or promoting content.

Growth hacking is *NOT* pushing anything onto someone else. It is about growing your audience and presenting activity across your channels. This shows that you're involved in your industry and communities and that you have a vested interest in what's going on. This will help you to build attraction and affinity toward your brand.

Offering a product or service that clients really *want* and care about is principal to the success of any campaign you may even be thinking of

launching. Product affinity is priceless. Placing your organization on these social spaces, web properties, and organic search results will assist with PR and allow you to gather feedback and input from your customers. This input is vital to continued growth of not only your channels, but your business as a whole.

You need to provide your visitors with value. Provide them with a resolution to their problem. Find out how you can help mitigate their pain points, and be responsible for giving them the answers they're looking for.

Redefine Growth

Every motive and desire you have to grow your audience, your affinity and your bottom line require growth hacking at some level. You can call it whatever you want. Growth Hacking is a culmination of all of the efforts outlined in this book. It is the goals that you set, the analytics to measure, and the overall plan to accomplish.

Another key ingredient to growth: failure. We cannot attain success without failure. Do not be discouraged if your initial efforts don't exactly generate accolades and bring golden clients to your doorstep. Learn from these lessons and fix what isn't working. Many times it takes strategy adjustments to figure out the best angle. Measure twice, cut once.

Growth is essential to any business. Whether it's growing the audience or the all mighty dollar, you want to grow right? So your efforts should be focused on what continues to create the growth.

Try to create something unique for your business. Keep in mind that you aren't reinventing anything, you are merely utilizing something that might have worked for someone else. What have you noticed, marketing-wise that you felt was compelling? Keep these ideas in mind for your marketing efforts.

For brick and mortar businesses, you can utilize a few ideas for growth. Encourage patrons to follow you on Facebook, Twitter, Instagram, or wherever your primary channels may be. Include your domain name on printed materials, vehicles (*if applicable*), or create placards with your social media URLs to place at your entrance and exits.

Gain attention by using the custom SnapChat Geofilters, run a campaign during a local event and have folks take their pictures inside or outside your business. Have customers post an image to their Instagram account and tag your account. Don't forget to come up with a good hashtag campaign and ask customers to use the hashtag in their posts. Avoid anything that could be spun as negative or inappropriate, keep your audience in mind.

Growth Hacking is a way to bring more attention to your business. Come up with some ideas on your own. Research some ideas and see if any other businesses have done something similar with success. Keep your focus on the client, after all, they are your number one marketing tool.

Notes & Takeaways

Notes & Takeaways

7

SEO TIPS & TRICKS

S earch Engine Optimization or SEO has become a necessity in one way or another for every website seeking success online. You can, of course, find someone, or a company that specializes in SEO and pay to appear higher in the Search Engine Result Pages. Just be sure that they are not getting you blacklisted from the Search Engines by using Blackhat techniques that the Search giants will absolutely penalize you for.

SEO Legends & Myths

Digital Marketing is not as esoteric as some agencies and consultants want you to believe. SEO is not an urban legend or secret witchcraft, although I do feel as though you need a superior understanding of what actual search optimization is. You can discover, learn and gain knowledge of best practices and guidelines that work well for your properties by research and educating yourself.

The myth is that you *have* to **pay** to get good results. However, that is just not true. Organic search results are more prevalent and possible than you might believe. Don't start stuffing your pages or profiles with keywords or phrases that you think will get you higher results. This can somewhat backfire and have the reverse effects, as search engines are very keen to these non-authentic tactics, not to mention it is annoying to your visitors. So in short, don't be foolish - be intelligent.

SEO You Need to Know

Proper optimization with SEO starts of course with your website content itself. You do not need crazy amounts of keywords, phrases, or meta descriptions to *get* great results. Meta descriptions can still be used to your advantage. When your site shows up in search engine result pages, the meta description will show as the truncated byline under your page title on the search results pages. The meta description can also be utilized by your social networks when you or someone else shares your page. Keep that in mind for gaining the attention of your customers, not the search engines.

Page title tag optimization is often either overlooked or misunderstood. The Page Title should ALWAYS be relevant to the content on the respective page. Too often I see sites that will place their company or organization name first in the title tag. Your first three words in every page title should be indicative of the pages' content. The title that you use is not only what shows in the search results, but also in social previews. With the possible exception of your home page, you do not need to include your business or organization name in the title tag. Think in regards to what words or phrase that someone might "Google" and hopefully they will land on your page as a result of their search.

As mentioned earlier under Social Media Optimization; the 2 or 3 sentences that you formulate should be nearly universal to remain consistent when describing your purpose or organizational ambitions.

These sentences should also be used in your website on your home page itself.

Don't create such diverse descriptions across your channels that you both confuse and contrive the opinions of your visitors. Although each page in your website truly needs its own description, consistency is the key in your content and your organizational voice on each page becomes the narrative focus. Although individually different, it is important to maintain a consistent tone across your entire site and various channels.

It is important to optimize your site content by using the first paragraph, or first few sentences on each page, or each post, to get your message across about what the visitor will find on that page, or what the post is about. Focus on key phrases that make the most valuable depiction of your content on each respective page. Do not bloat your content, do not insert keywords that don't actually define what each individual page is about. Content integrity not only builds customer trust but creates valuable organic search optimization. The content on your pages and posts should have a human feel, and not sound stagnant or make a hollow statement.

Websites and social networks are the major media outlets of the world. Computers and devices get more focus and attention than televisions or radio. You have to create a personality for your brand and convey that persona which reaches your prospects wherever you represent your brand. These are *your* channels and should be tuned-in to your customers, prospects and visitors.

Going Mobile

An imperative aspect that not only provides ease of use for your visitors but is also significant to Search Engine Result Pages: mobile-friendly webpages. If your site is not mobile-friendly, or responsive yet – you better step it up. Google and Bing have already begun giving favor and precedence to mobile-friendly websites over their desktop-only counterparts. So if your competitors have a mobile-friendly site, and you don't; they are already ahead of the game, and you are behind the ball.

You can take advantage of many frameworks, toolkits, and website templates that are available for responsive websites. Many of these are free or relatively inexpensive, and seemingly easy to find. WordPress and Bootstrap are both great examples of where you can start with a mobile-friendly website. If you already have a responsive site, great – you've already made a huge step in the right direction.

Google Knows

Google provides many guides and how-to steps that can be very helpful for your website success. One of the best resources for Search Engine Optimization is, of course, Google themselves. Whether you're a diehard fan, or you cannot stand Google, you cannot ignore the fact that they essentially have the most reliable advice when it comes to Search Engine Optimization, as well as utilizing your site intelligently.

Take a few minutes and research Google's own SEO info here: ***j2c.me/Goo-SEO***

Google actually provides a mobile-friendly test tool here: ***j2c.me/Goo-MF*** - Simply type in your URL to analyze a web page and generate a report if the page is mobile-friendly and the tool will give you optimization recommendations. Make sure that you take some time clicking around the other resources that Google provides in the tab bar. In particular, check out **Documentation > Mobile SEO**, and read through the various sections on the side navigation.

Optimum Submission

Optimizing your site for the best user experience and search engine results is a seriously important aspect to ensure your online success. But getting to the search engines is another crucial step. You have a great website with plenty of magnificent content, and your social media channels are all up to par and on point.

Did you know that you can actually inform the search engines that your website is ready to be indexed the engine? There used to be a time where you had wait weeks, maybe even a couple of months before you could experience any sort of mediocre organic search engine results. You would have called someone like me to handle your search engine optimization and submissions because I know the secrets to getting those results fast, right? Well, the simple answer is yes and no.

Yes, I do know some information about search optimization and submissions that not every business around the corner knows much about. Yes, I do know how to get your website indexed within a couple of hours and have you showing in Google results in about a day. I am not saying you'll be number one overnight, I am just saying that I can assure you that your site will be indexed and show in Google results in some way. I'll explain more about gaining better results.

So now, the NO answer... No, you do not have pay anyone an exorbitant amount of money to get your website into Google. No, you do not have to wait for weeks to get your website indexed or 'spidered' or the 'robots' to come and index your site. No, I am not pulling your leg, and yes, I am going to tell you how to do this yourself.

Google and Bing have webmaster tools that are built to help you get your website content indexed into the engines, and also ensure that you don't have any significant errors or roadblocks that keep you from getting into results. Yahoo! is part of the Bing network, so submitting and managing via the Bing tools also powers Yahoo!

There is a process that is explained on the respective submission pages for each engine. You will want to go through the optimization process outlined earlier in this book thoroughly prior to submitting your site to the search engines. Once you feel like your site and content are ready to onboard with Google and Bing, it's time to make some noise. The following are simple instructions for submitting your site to Google and Bing webmaster tools. These tools and services will aid in your search engine results and help you to maintain an optimized website.

Bing Webmaster Tools - *j2c.me/Bing-WebTools* -
If you don't already have an account with Bing Webmaster Tools, create one now. This is similar to the Google Webmaster Tools – *j2c.me/Goo-WebTools*, and will be helpful for your Bing and Yahoo! submissions, etc. As of this writing, Bing includes a $100 advertising credit free for signing up. Bing also provides some excellent guidelines, again much like Google, that you can benefit from.

Bing Webmaster Guidelines - *j2c.me/Bing-Guidelines* -

These guidelines cover a broad range of topics and are intended to help your content be found and indexed by Bing. These guidelines will not cover every instance, nor provide prescriptive actions specific to every website.

You should read our self-help documents and follow the Bing Webmaster Blog. In your Bing Webmaster Tools account, you will find SEO Reports and the SEO Analyzer tool for on-demand scanning of individual pages. Both resources will offer basic guidance and recommendations in regards to site optimizations that you can apply to your site. [10]

---

[10] *Excerpts from Bing.com*

Quick Bing Submission, go to: ***j2c.me/Bing-Submit***

Taking some time to learn about the Bing Webmaster Tools will not only increase your knowledge of search engine optimization, but also the value in optimizing your site as it pertains to greater results for searches. Creating a sitemap and submitting it to Bing is a powerful process in and of itself. I will touch on how to create a sitemap and submit to the engines toward the end of this chapter.

Google Webmaster Guidelines - ***j2c.me/Goo-Guidelines*** -

Following the General Guidelines will help Google find, index, and rank your site.

Ensure that all pages on the site can be reached by a link from another findable page. The referring link should include either text or, for images, an alt attribute, that is relevant to the target page.

We strongly encourage you to pay very close attention to the Quality Guidelines on this page, which outline some of the illicit practices that may lead to a site being removed entirely from the Google index or otherwise affected by an algorithmic or manual spam action. If a site has been affected by a spam action, it may no longer show up in results on Google.com or on any of Google's partner sites.[11]

---

[11] *Excerpts from Google.com*

Quick Google Submission, go to: *j2c.me/Goo-Submit*

At the very least, you want to submit your homepage URL to the engines. This will let them know that your site exists, and eventually their bots will crawl your entire site and index interior pages without any further submissions. However, the most powerful intent is to ensure that all pages in your site are submitted and that the individual engines accept the submissions and will start to index as soon as possible.

It is important and helpful to have a sitemap.xml file for your site. Assuming that you are using a CMS for your site, it most likely creates a sitemap, has a plugin or module to create a sitemap, or at the very least – easily indexed content. Look into the options available for your CMS.

If you do not have a sitemap, you need to generate one. This is one of the ways you can ping the search engines and let them know to index your site, as well as how often you plan to update the site. This helps the engines approximate how often to check for new content.

Although it is better to have a dynamically created sitemap from within your CMS, you can also have one generated for your site. This will certainly help for initial submissions of your site.

One of the options that I use is *j2c.me/XMLSitemap* - this site will automatically crawl the pages of your site and create a sitemap file for you. You can download the XML file and then upload to your web server, and then you can directly submit the sitemap.xml URL to Google or Bing.

Here are the URLs that you will need to place into your browser to submit your newly created sitemap to Google and Bing, without uploading any file to your server!

Google Sitemap Submission:

__google.com/ping?sitemap=http://YOURSITE.com/sitemap.xml__

Bing Sitemap Submission:

__bing.com/ping?sitemap=http://YOURSITE.com/sitemap.xml__

Obviously, you will replace *YOURSITE* with your own URL. When you click Enter and submit your sitemap to the respective search engine, you should get a result page showing that your sitemap was submitted. Voila! You have submitted your site to the search giants!

There are other options for submitting your site as well. Here is another great resource for submitting your site to other various directories and sites for free, as well as some other helpful SEO and marketing solutions: *__j2c.me/JCC-SEO__* - click on 'Free Tools' and 'Submit Free.' There are a lot of great paid services available as well[12].

Taking your time to go through all of the Webmaster tools can increase your site's presence in search results, and teach you how to better formulate your website and content. Bing has a great keyword

---

[12] *This is part of an affiliate program that I use, I make a commission on sales.*

lookup that can help you measure the competitiveness of given keywords and phrases.

Make sure that you also search through Google and Bing for your own results. Look up your company, your products, and what you are optimizing for. This will help you to understand where you are showing up in results. You may also want to open incognito windows so that the engines don't show you tracked results. Then you can view results as others see them.

Once you realize the potential for organic results, you can optimize each page, and each post. Focus on your post and article titles. The titles that become the page titles should be relevant to the content on the respective URL. This is the number one optimization key to ensure that your page or content is indexed properly and relative to the canonical page.

Search engines and visitors should be kept in the front of your mind when optimizing. What are you creating? What terms will someone potentially search for and find your page? What is it that you are wanting them to find?

Another idea is to look up the terms or title that you want to use. Take a look at the competitive nature of the phrase you want to use. Use this as a measuring device to determine if you have a strong title. The next step is to make sure you repeat the title, but not verbatim, throughout your page content.

Notes & Takeaways

Notes & Takeaways

_____

_____

_____

_____

_____

_____

_____

_____

_____

_____

_____

_____

_____

RESOURCES

Although we do our best to check for errors, misspellings, dead links, etc. there are occasional issues that pop up. If you find any errors or issues, please let us know – *books@connettconsulting.com*.

Here are some of the tools, apps, and services that I utilize besides the ones listed in the book. These include: **Pinterest, Anchor, GhostCodes, Grab, Google Apps for Business, Google Photos, Typorama, Instapload, Videorama, Giant Square, Crowdfire, Slack, InsTrack, Spark Post, Ripl**, and **Skype**.

To make it a little easier, here are the URL's from the book in one place:

Excerpts from Wikipedia - http://wikipedia.org
Buffer – http://j2c.me/JC-Buffer
Hootsuite - http://j2c.me/JC-Hootsuite
Later - http://j2c.me/IG-Later
Facebook Business Manager - http://j2c.me/FB-BusinessManager
IFTTT - http://j2c.me/JC-IFTTT
Excerpt from Google Developers -
http://developers.google.com/webmasters/mobile-sites/#why
Excerpt from Google Blog -
http://webmasters.googleblog.com/2014/11/helping-users-find-mobile-friendly-pages.html
Facebook Pages Help - http://j2c.me/FB-PagesHelp

SnapChat Geofilters - http://j2c.me/SC-Geofilters

Twitter Analytics - http://j2c.me/TW-Analytics

Facebook Analytics - http://j2c.me/FB-Analytics

Pinterest Analytics - http://j2c.me/PIN-Analytics

Instagram Analytics - Iconosquare - http://j2c.me/IS-Analytics

Google Analytics - http://j2c.me/Goo-Analytics

Google Tag Manager - http://j2c.me/Goo-TM

Google Analytics Goals - http://j2c.me/Goo-Goals

Google Social Analytics - http://j2c.me/Goo-SA

The Definitive Guide to Growth Hacking - http://j2c.me/JC-GH

Google SEO - http://j2c.me/Goo-SEO

Google Mobile-Friendly Tool - http://j2c.me/Goo-MF

Bing Webmaster Tools - http://j2c.me/Bing-WebTools

Bing Webmaster Guidelines - http://j2c.me/Bing-Guidelines

Bing Submission - http://j2c.me/Bing-Submit

Google Webmaster Tools – http://j2c.me/Goo-WebTools

Google Webmaster Guidelines - http://j2c.me/Goo-Guidelines

Google Submission - http://j2c.me/Goo-Submit

XML Sitemap - http://j2c.me/XMLSitemap

SEO Tools & Services - http://j2c.me/JCC-SEO

Google Sitemap Submission -
http://google.com/ping?sitemap=http://YOURSITE.com/sitemap.xml

Bing Sitemap Submission -
http://bing.com/ping?sitemap=http://YOURSITE.com/sitemap.xml

ABOUT THE AUTHOR

Christian Connett is a Digital Marketing Architect, Strategist and an Adjunct College Instructor with over 16 years of experience on the web helping small and mid-sized organizations achieve online success. Christian creates strategies for Search Engine Optimization, Social Media, Content Marketing, UI/UX, and Information Architecture.

Christian has created successful strategies for individuals and organizations of all sizes including Partnerships, Limited Liability Companies, Associations, Financial Institutions, Non-Profits, and Fortune 500 companies.

Christian spends his free time enjoying time with his daughters and listening to his eclectic music collection. He is also an outdoor enthusiast.

Christian is available for speaking engagements utilizing his personally developed curriculum based on the Principles of Digital Marketing and the 7 Keys. Christian is also available for advanced and strategic speaking engagements and coaching seminars. Contact Connett Consulting at *info@christianconnett.com* for more information.

Socialize with Christian

LinkedIn	@ChristianConnett
Facebook	@JChristianConnett
Twitter	@eSolutions
Instagram	@ChristianConnett
SnapChat	@ChristianConnet
Tumblr	@ChristianConnett
Email	cc@christianconnett.com
Forvera	facebook.com/ForveraMedia

THANK YOU FOR YOUR SUPPORT

forvera